Make Origami
BIRDS

by Ruth Owen

PowerKiDS press
New York

Published in 2018 by **The Rosen Publishing Group, Inc.**
29 East 21st Street, New York, NY 10010

CATALOGING-IN-PUBLICATION DATA
Names: Owen, Ruth.
Title: Make origami birds / Ruth Owen.
Description: New York : PowerKids Press, 2018. | Series: Animal kingdom origami |
    Includes index.
Identifiers: ISBN 9781499433524 (pbk.) | ISBN 9781499433463 (library bound) |
    ISBN 9781499433340 (6 pack)
Subjects: LCSH: Origami--Juvenile literature. | Birds in art--Juvenile literature.
Classification: LCC TT872.5 O94 2018 | DDC 736'.982--dc23

First Edition

Produced for Rosen by Ruth Owen Books

Designer: Emma Randall
Photo Credits: Courtesy of Ruth Owen Books and Shutterstock.

Manufactured in the United States of America
CPSIA Compliance Information: Batch BS17PK: For Further Information contact Rosen Publishing, New York, New York at 1-800-237-9932.

Contents

What Is a Bird?

There are more than 10,000 different **species**, or types, of birds. They come in many shapes and colors. They also range in size from the tiny bee hummingbird, that's just 2 inches (5 cm) long, to an ostrich that can grow to be 9 feet (3 m) tall!

Macaw parrot

Birds have six main characteristics.

Birds have wings and most species are able to fly. Some types of birds, such as ostriches and penguins, are flightless, however.

Ostrich

Bee hummingbird

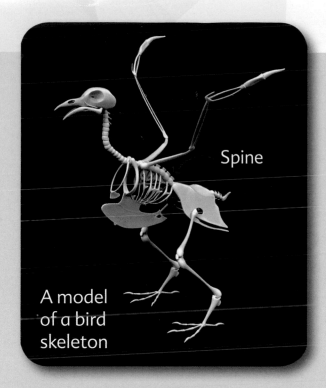

Spine

A model of a bird skeleton

Birds are **vertebrates**, which means they have a spine, or backbone. Most birds have a lightweight skeleton which reduces their body weight for flying.

Birds are **endothermic**, or warm-blooded. This means a bird's body is able to **regulate** its inner body temperature. Even if its environment is very hot or cold, a bird's inner body temperature stays the same.

Beak

Toucan

Feathers

All birds have beaks and feathers.

No matter how big or small, every bird begins its life by hatching from an egg.

Robin eggs inside a nest

Ready to discover more? Then grab some origami paper and let's get folding and learning all about birds!

Chick and Egg: It's Time to Hatch!

Just as birds come in many sizes, so do their eggs. The eggs of the tiny bee hummingbird are smaller than an M&M. The largest egg is laid by the ostrich. It can weigh more than 3 pounds (1.4 kg)!

The chicks of some bird species, for example robins and owls, are helpless when they hatch from their eggs. The baby birds cannot walk or see. Their parents must bring them food for the first few weeks of their lives. Other chicks, such as the babies of ducks, ostriches, and chickens, can run around and peck at food within a day of hatching.

Chick

Ostrich egg

Chicken egg

FOLD A HATCHING CHICK

You will need:
- A square piece of paper that's yellow on one side and white on the other
- A black marker

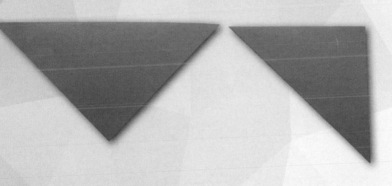

STEP 1:

Place the paper colored side down, fold in half diagonally, and crease. Then fold in half again.

STEP 2:

Turn the paper so the longest side is at the bottom. Fold the top flap of the paper back on itself, and crease.

STEP 3:

Now open out the top pocket of paper on the right side. Gently squash the pocket and fold it back down to form a square.

STEP 4:

Turn the model over. Now fold in the right side along the dotted line, and crease. Open out the top pocket of paper and then gently squash and fold it back down to form a square.

7

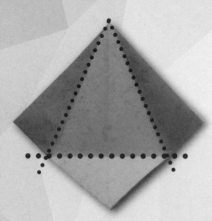

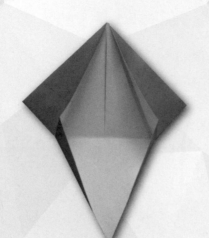

STEP 5:
Turn the model so that the open points are at the top. Fold both sides and the bottom into the center along the dotted lines, and crease. Then unfold.

STEP 6:
Now pull open the top layer of paper. Then gently squash it back down to form a diamond shape, and crease.

STEP 7:
Fold up the bottom point of the diamond so it lays flat against the model.

STEP 8:
Turn the model over. Fold down the top layer of paper, and crease. Your model should look like this.

STEP 9:
Now fold down the two points at the top of the model to make the chick's wings, and crease.

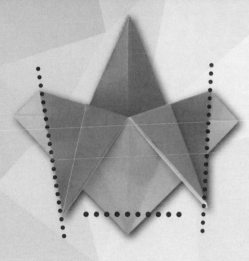

STEP 10:
Fold the three points behind the model, along the dotted lines, and crease.

STEP 11:
Fold down the top point to make the chick's head.

STEP 12:
Finally make two small folds at the pointed end of the chick's head to create its beak. Fold back the corners of its head to round off the shape.

Draw on eyes, and your hatching chick is complete!

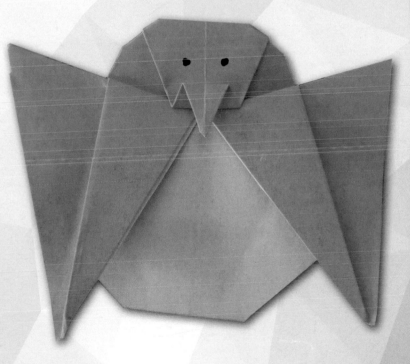

Hummingbirds: Precision Flyers

Hummingbirds are precision flyers that drink nectar from flowers. In order to feed from a flower, the tiny bird must hover in one place. As it hovers, a ruby-throated hummingbird beats its wings more than 50 times each second!

FOLD A HUMMINGBIRD

You will need:
• A square piece of paper in your choice of color
• Scissors

Step 1:

To begin making your hummingbird, follow steps 1 to 4 of the chick and egg project on page 7. Your model should now look like this.

Ruby-throated hummingbird

Open section

Open section

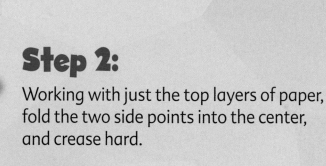

Step 2:

Working with just the top layers of paper, fold the two side points into the center, and crease hard.

Step 3:

Turn the model over and repeat step 2. Next, fold down the top point, and crease hard.

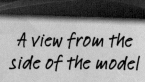

A view from the side of the model

Step 4:

Now unfold the three folds you made in step 3 and open up the top layer of paper. Your model will look a little like a bird's beak.

Next, gently squash and flatten the model to create a diamond shape.

Turn the model over and it should look like this.

Step 5:

Now repeat what you did in step 4, unfolding the top layer of paper, and then squashing and flattening the paper into a diamond shape.

You should now have two leg-like points at the bottom of your model.

Step 6:

Turn the model 90 degrees clockwise. Working with just the top layer of paper, fold up the bottom point into the center.

Then turn the model over and fold up the bottom point.

Now, working with just the top layer of paper, fold down the top point.

Finally, turn the model over and fold down the remaining top point.

Step 7:

Turn the model so the two leg-like points are at the bottom.

Next fold up the left-hand point. Crease hard and then unfold.

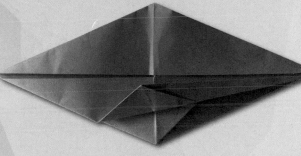

Leg-like points

FOLD A BALD EAGLE

You will need:
- A square piece of paper that's black on one side and white on the other

STEP 1:

Place the paper black side down, fold along the dotted line, crease, and unfold.

STEP 2:

Fold the two side points into the center, and crease.

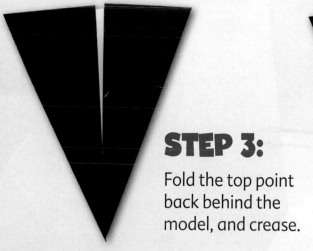

STEP 3:

Fold the top point back behind the model, and crease.

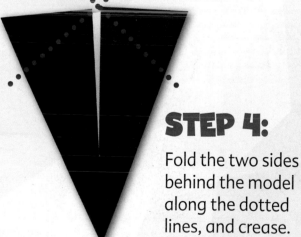

STEP 4:

Fold the two sides behind the model along the dotted lines, and crease. Then unfold again.

Diamond shape

Your model should look like this.

STEP 5:

Now lift up point A. Gently fold and squash the paper down so it creates a diamond shape, and crease well.

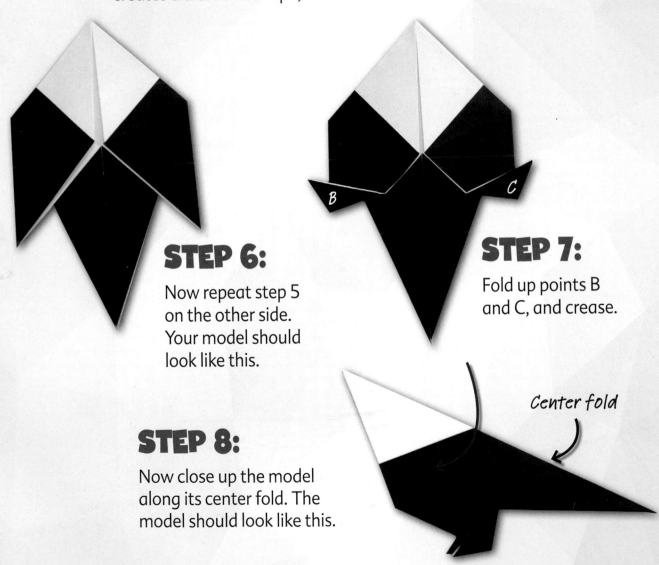

STEP 6:

Now repeat step 5 on the other side. Your model should look like this.

STEP 7:

Fold up points B and C, and crease.

Center fold

STEP 8:

Now close up the model along its center fold. The model should look like this.

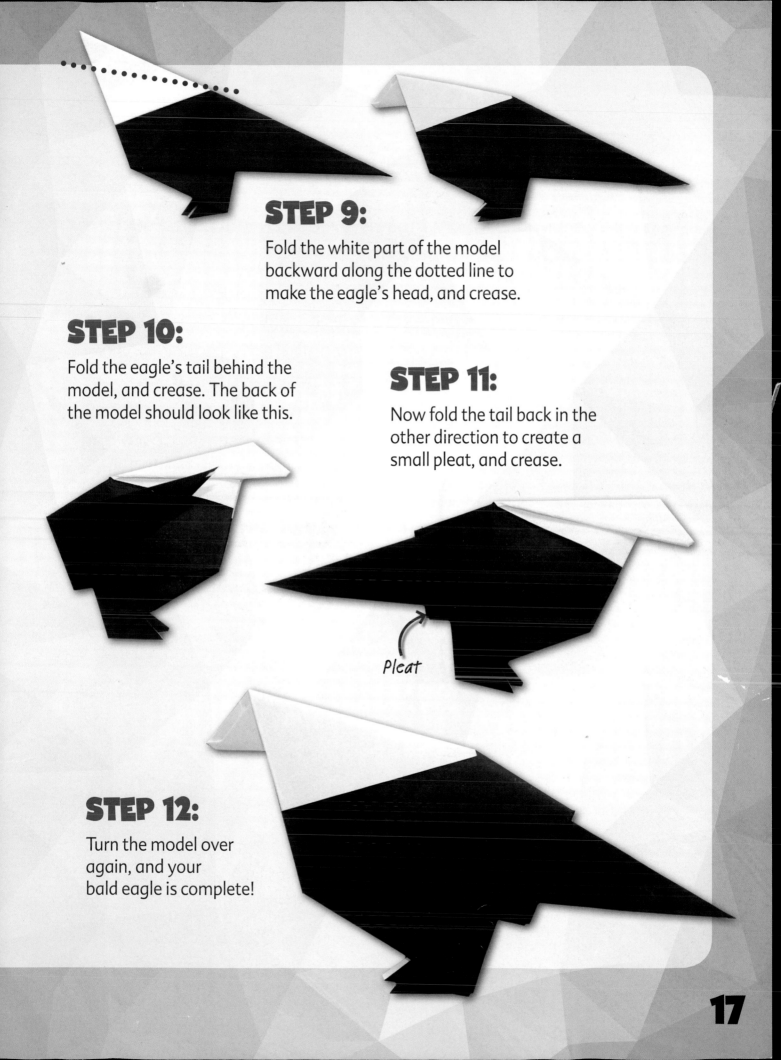

STEP 9:

Fold the white part of the model backward along the dotted line to make the eagle's head, and crease.

STEP 10:

Fold the eagle's tail behind the model, and crease. The back of the model should look like this.

STEP 11:

Now fold the tail back in the other direction to create a small pleat, and crease.

Pleat

STEP 12:

Turn the model over again, and your bald eagle is complete!

Parrots: Fantastic Feathers

All birds have bodies and wings covered with feathers. Feathers help birds fly, and keep them warm and dry.

Macaws are large parrots with very brightly colored feathers. When a macaw chick hatches from its egg, however, it is covered in pale, fluffy feathers called down. During its first few weeks, though, the chick loses its down and small spikes, called pin feathers, start to grow. Then, red, blue, yellow, or green feathers soon **unfurl** from the pin feathers.

Macaw chicks

Spiky pin feathers

Fluffy down

Adult macaw

Colorful feathers unfurling

Macaw feathers

FOLD A PARROT

You will need:
- A square piece of colorful paper
- Scissors

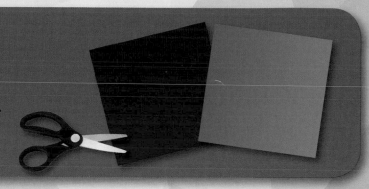

Step 1:

Fold the paper in half, crease well, and then unfold. Fold the paper in half again, in the opposite direction, crease well, and then unfold.

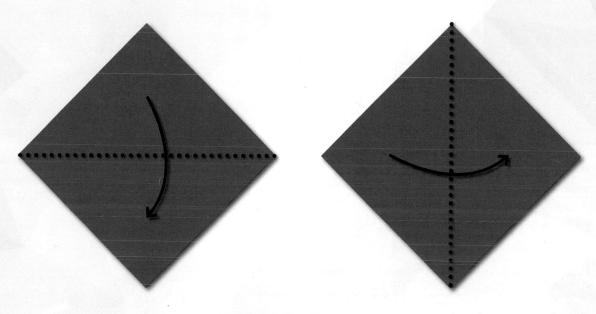

Step 2:

Fold the top and bottom points into the center crease along the dotted lines. Crease well, and then unfold.

Step 3:

Now fold the top and bottom points into the center crease in the opposite direction. Crease well, and then unfold.

Beak-like pocket

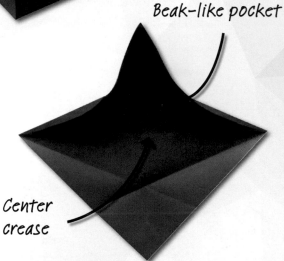

Center crease

Step 4:

Now gently fold the top half of the paper into the center crease while allowing the top point to create a beak-like pocket. Then squash the pocket and fold it to the right-hand side of the model.

Squashed beak-like pocket

Repeat on the bottom half of the model.

Step 5:

Turn the model over. Fold down the top half along the center crease.

Step 6:

Turn the model by 90 degrees clockwise. To make the parrot's head, fold down the top point, crease well, and then unfold.

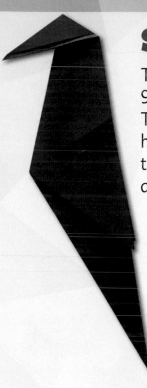

Back of head

Open out the head section of the model.

Then reverse fold the head using the creases you've just made.

Your parrot's head should now look like this.

Step 7:

Fold down the tip of the head to make the parrot's beak.

Step 8:

To complete the parrot, cut some feather shapes into the parrot's tail.

21

Turkeys: Feathers for Showing Off

In the world of birds, males are often more colorful than females. They may also have special feathers that they use for showing off to females during the **mating season**.

Turkeys are large birds that live wild in forests. When a male turkey wants to impress a female, he struts toward her and makes gobbling noises. He also puffs out the feathers on his body. His long tail feathers fan out to create a dramatic display.

Fan of tail feathers

Puffed-up body

Female turkey

Male turkey

FOLD A TURKEY

You will need:
- Two square pieces of paper in your choice of colors
- Scissors
- Glue or tape

STEP 1:

To make the turkey's body, fold a piece of paper in half diagonally, crease, and unfold.

STEP 2:

Now fold the two side points in so they meet in the center, and crease well.

STEP 3:

Repeat Step 2 by folding both sides of the model into the center again, and crease well.

STEP 4:

Turn the model over. Fold down the top point to meet the bottom of the model, and crease.

Then fold the point back up again to create the turkey's head.

STEP 5:

Now turn the model by 90 degrees. Fold the model in half by bringing together points A and B behind the model.

Then gently pull up the neck part of the model.

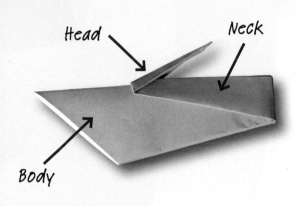

STEP 6:

Fold down the point of the turkey's head to make its wobbly wattle.

Fold in the left-hand side of the turkey's body. Make a small cut into the body that measures about ¼ of an inch (1 cm). Then unfold.

Cut in here

STEP 7:

To make the turkey's tail, take the second piece of paper and fold it into a series of pleats. Each pleat should be the width of the cut that's now in the turkey's body.

Once all the pleats are made, gather them together into a narrow bunch. Fold the bunch in half lengthwise.

Halfway point

Bunch of pleats

STEP 8:

Now slot the bunch of pleats through the cut in the turkey's body, so that half the pleats are on either side of the body. Adjust the length of the cut if you need to.

Your model should now look like this.

STEP 9:

Fan out the pleats on either side of the turkey's body. Use a little tape or glue to hold the pleats in the perfect position. Your origami turkey is complete!

Emperor Penguins: Life in the Freezer

Emperor penguins live in the Antarctic—one of the most extreme habitats on Earth. Here, temperatures can drop to -22°F (-30°C) and freezing blizzards blow at more than 100 miles per hour (160 km/h). Emperor penguins are well **insulated** against the cold by large amounts of body fat and layers of overlapping feathers.

After a female emperor lays an egg she heads off to sea to hunt. Her mate **incubates** the egg, keeping it warm on his feet. As they care for their eggs, the thousands of males in a **colony** huddle together to keep warm. They take turns standing on the freezing outside of the huddle and inside the toasty warm center.

Father penguin

Chick

FOLD A PENGUIN

You will need:
• A square piece of paper that's black on one side and white on the other

Step 1:

Place the paper white side down. Fold in half diagonally, and crease.

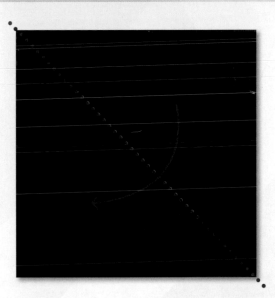

Step 2:

Fold back the right-hand point so that it meets the model's left-hand edge. Crease well.

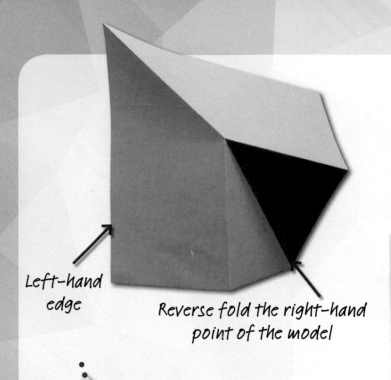

Left-hand edge

Reverse fold the right-hand point of the model

Step 3:

Unfold the crease you've just made. Open out the model, and using the creases you've just made, reverse fold the right-hand point so that it folds inside the model.

The right-hand point is now folded and tucked inside the model

Step 4:

Now fold the left-hand edge forward along the dotted line, and crease.

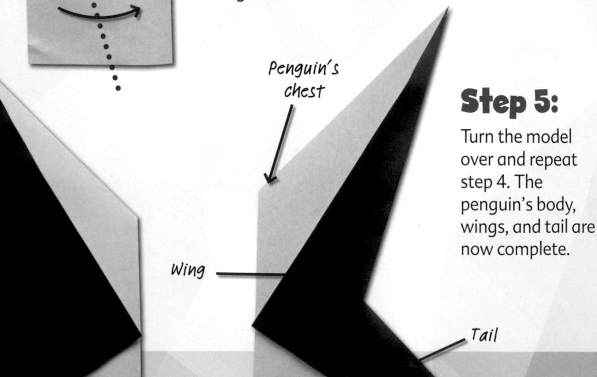

Penguin's chest

Wing

Step 5:

Turn the model over and repeat step 4. The penguin's body, wings, and tail are now complete.

Tail

Step 6:

To make the penguin's head, fold down the top point of the model so that the top edge of the head is parallel to the bottom edge of the model. Crease hard and then unfold.

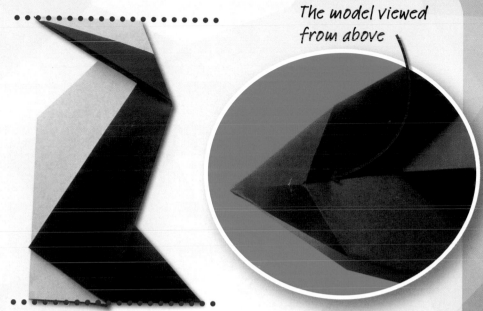

The model viewed from above

Open out the head section of the model.

Using the creases you've just made, reverse fold the head so that it folds down over the body. The black hood of the penguin's head should now be tucked around either side of the white chest.

Step 7:

Gently open out the bottom of the model so your penguin can stand, and your model is complete.

Glossary

colony
A large group of animals that live together.

endothermic
Warm-blooded and able to maintain a constant inner body temperature.

incubates
Keeps an egg warm so the chick inside develops and hatches.

insulated
Protected by fat or by layers of material to stop heat loss.

mating season
The time of year when a particular species of animal mates.

prey
An animal that is hunted by another animal as food.

regulate
To adjust the temperature up or down to keep it at the same level.

regurgitates
Coughs up (or vomits up) something that has already been eaten.

rodents
A large group of small animals that includes mice, rats, hamsters, squirrels, and prairie dogs.

species
One type of living thing. The members of a species look alike and can produce young together.

talons
Sharp claws on the feet of a bird of prey, such as an eagle or owl.

vertebrates
Animals with spines, or backbones, and a skeleton of other bones.

unfurl
Spread out from a rolled-up state.

waterfowl
Birds, such as ducks and geese, that spend lots of time on water.

Websites

Due to the changing nature of internet links, PowerKids Press has developed an online list of websites related to the subject of this book. This site is updated regularly. Please use this link to access the list:

www.powerkidslinks.com/ako/birds

Index